Jean Vanier

I meet JESUS

He tells me "I Love you"

Story of the Love of God
through the Bible -

This book is for you
my brother, my sister.

It speaks of JESUS and his message
but it is written especially to help you meet JESUS.

If you want-
stop and spend time with just one picture
one that speaks to your heart and gives you peace
or remain with one text that nourishes your heart.

If you have difficulties
share with a friend of JESUS
he or she can help you a lot
but especially pray to JESUS
he will enlighten you.

Little by little- it takes time-
JESUS will reveal to you how much he watches over you
and loves you

he calls you to follow him
so that you may do something beautiful
with your life and bear much fruit

the world needs you
the Church needs you
JESUS needs you
they need your love and your light.

know, my brother, my sister
that there is a hidden place in your heart
where JESUS lives
this is a deep secret
you are called to live

Let JESUS live in you,
go forward with him!

I feel so lonely, unwanted, useless
closed up in myself
such anger and sadness in my heart
disgusted with life and with myself.

One day I meet JESUS
      he looks at me,
      he smiles at me,
      he touches me.
      I can tell he loves me
      just as I am with my difficulties

           my heart rejoices
           a new source of life flows within me
           a small light burns in my heart

Yes, JESUS
   I can tell
   you are really my friend
   you love me and understand me
   you trust me
            and I love you

   From now on, I will never be alone.

And JESUS guides me
he is my good shepherd
he calls me by my name

       and says:

     "Be not afraid
     in all your difficulties
     I am watching over you

        trust
     for I am with you always
     but you must make many efforts
     and go forward with me "

" I am leading you to a land of peace and of rest
  I am preparing a wonderful feast for you
  I nourish you with my Body and my Blood
  I nourish you with my heart
  I give you new strength
  I give you my spirit "

" I love each one of you so much
  that I give my life for you
  I want each one of you to be free and happy "

Jesus brings me into the family of God

He brings me to his father
who is also my father, Daddy

Our Father

so JESUS is my big brother
I am united to him and to the father
through the Holy Spirit which he gives me
in baptism.

JESUS also brings me to
Mary, his Mother
she is also my mother, mommy.
I love her and trust her
she is so much like JESUS.

JeSUS brings me into the family of the Father
        He gives me new brothers and sisters
        in community

I am happy to be part of
        the larger family of God now
        which is spread throughout the world

                    that's the Church.

And in the family of God
JESUS gives us priests
       they speak of JESUS
       they celebrate Mass, the Eucharist
       they give us the Body of JESUS to eat
         and his Blood to drink

In the name of JESUS they forgive us our sins
they help us live the Good News of JESUS

Jesus teaches me to pray

I look at him
he looks at me

It's so good to be together!
he says: "I love you
as the Father loves me,
remain in my love"

With JESUS I am happy and relaxed.

And JESUS says to me:
"When you pray to my Father, say:

My Father, Our Father, daddy!
you are so wonderful, so good, so strong!
Oh, if only everyone could know you
and do what you ask!

May your kingdom come!
May your will be done!

cf Matthew 6,9-13

"Father, I am hungry
　　the world is hungry!
　　　　I need you!
　　　　We all need you!
　　　　The world needs you!

Come!
Give us this day
our daily bread!"

" Father, forgive me my sins
           forgive us our sins
           wash all our faults away

           Heal us! "

"Father, protect us
    deliver us from evil
    deliver us from the evil one"

Then JESUS promises me something:

"Whatever you ask the Father
in my Name
he will give it to you
Yes, he will give it to you.
Trust!"

cf John 15, 16

And JESUS looks at Mary, his mother, with tenderness

he says to her:

"Hail, Mary, full of grace"

I pray with him:

"Hail, Mary, full of grace"

Jesus teaches me how to live

JESUS looks at me lovingly
and says: "Come with me, follow me.
              We will live together"

I go with him and I see how he lives:
              He is a friend of the poor
He is so kind and gentle with the lonely ones,
              the little ones, and all unhappy people.

JeSUS calls all the poor to him:

"Come to me
all you who are weary and heavy-laden
and I will give you rest
learn from me
for I am meek and humble of heart "

cf Matthew 11,28

Jesus gives bread to the hungry

cf Mark 6,41

Everywhere he goes, JESUS speaks of his Father
he always announces the Truth
he is really the Light of the world
he detests what is not true

JESUS comforts the broken-hearted
he loves to live close to them

cf Luke 7,12

Jesus heals the wounded and the sick

cf Luke 5.17

He calls little children to him

he kisses them
he blesses them
because he loves them

he says to me :
"If you do not become like one of these little one
-full of trust and simplicity,
you cannot enter the Kingdom of Heaven"

cf Matthew 18,2

JESUS tells me a story
to show how good his Father is
and how much he forgives us:

" There is a man who has two sons
the younger of them asks his father
for his share of money
and he leaves on a journey into a distant country.
There he wastes all his money
on loose living"

"Now when he has spent everything,
famine invades the country
he has nothing- nothing to eat
no work
        he feeds the pigs
        but he is so hungry
        he would like to eat the scraps
        that the pigs are eating

        he begins to long for his father's house"

54

" He decides to go back to his father
       who is waiting for him
       for he still loves his son

When he sees him coming his heart leaps with joy
       he runs to greet him
       he takes him in his arms
       and hugs him

The young son cries and says :
       Daddy, I have sinned against heaven
       and against you. I am sorry, forgive me !

          they embrace each other
          happy to be reconciled. "

" the father is so happy to see his son again
that he calls for a big celebration.
Everyone rejoices
the son who was lost, has been found!
he who was dead, has come to life again!

only his older brother is angry
because he is jealous "

cf Luke 15

Jesus why have you come into our world ?

JESUS tells me that the Father sends him into the world
to save everyone
reconciling them with him
and making them his beloved children

The Father sends JESUS
        because he loves
        all the men and women
        of the earth

he sends him to announce the good, good news:
        God loves us
        just as we are
we are no longer left alone with our difficulties,
        anguish, handicaps,
everything does not end with death
we are made to live forever
        together with JESUS
and that life begins right now.

The Father sends JESUS
      to free all men and women
      from their prisons of selfishness
            guilt
            jealousy
            oppression
            violence
            death
            evil

Yes, he comes to save us and to free us

The Father sends JESUS
        to be Peace and Reconciliation
        in a world of conflict and war
        to be compassion
        in a world of suffering and misery

Jesus comes to forgive us
        all our faults, our sins
        our cowardice and indifference
he does not come to judge or to condemn

Jesus comes
        to transform our hearts
        which are selfish and hard
        to teach us to love and to share
        and to build a world that is more just,
        more beautiful, more friendly

                that's the Church!

JESUS comes
to invite all men and women
from all countries and races
to the great celebration of the Father

so that all may be ONE in him,
the King of Love and of Light.

72

And JESUS looks at me lovingly
and says:" Be like me
filled with kindness
be courageous
be my hands, my face and my heart
as I am the hands, the face and
the heart of my Father
As the Father sent me
I also send you
go announce the good news of Peace
tell everyone that God is love
liberate hardened hearts
forgive as I forgive
love as I love
struggle against evil as I struggle
against evil."

The bishop in the name of JESUS confirms us
for he is the father of the diocese
he sends us forth to announce the good news
and to serve JESUS and our brothers
and sisters, especially the poorest
Through the sacrament of confirmation
we receive a new strength from the Holy Spirit
to be witnesses of JESUS

The bishop also makes new priests

Jesus teaches me his way of life:
the beatitudes

cf Matthew 5

"Live poorly and simply
do not seek to become rich
find your security in me
I am your wealth and your peace

then you are happy
and blessed of my Father"

"Be gentle and humble of heart
      even with those who are unkind
      or nasty to you

            then you will be happy
            and blessed of my Father"

" Do not worry when you suffer
                    when you cry
     I will comfort you
     I will wipe away each one of your tears

     then you will be happy
     and blessed of my Father "

" Thirst and hunger for the kingdom of God,
Yearn that his will be done on earth as it is in heaven
pray and struggle just where you are
for a more friendly world
where the poor are honored

think of those who are suffering far away
and all those who are struggling against evil in the world
pray for them
live for them

then you will be happy
and blessed of my Father "

" Be kind with those who are lonely and rejected
   with those who are sad and in distress
   especially the poorest and the weakest
   share your life with them

I am hidden in their hearts
and whatever you do unto them
                you do unto me
they will help you
they will change your heart of stone
                into a heart of love.

                then you will be happy
                and blessed of my Father "

" May your heart be pure and transparent
like spring water

then you will be happy
and blessed of my Father "

" Seek always and everywhere to be peace-makers

then you will be happy
and blessed of my Father "

" If you are kind
   if you love me and try to do what I say
         you will be laughed at
         you will be pushed
         you will be persecuted

            do not worry
            do not be afraid
            I am with you

            then you are happy
            and blessed of my Father"

I say to JESUS

" but it is hard to love, to give
                to always forgive,
                to live as you say
I try but I can't
I often fail
so quickly I become discouraged
I become lazy
and just think of myself "

JESUS smiles at me:

" Yes, for you all alone, it is impossible
  but nothing is impossible for God
  I am here to help you and to forgive you.
          I forgive you through my priests
          in the sacrament of reconciliation
          In that way, you still remain my friend."

"But most important of all,
      eat my Body
      drink my Blood

      So I live in you
      and you live in me

      I give you my heart to love with
      I give you a new strength
            to struggle against evil
            in yourself and in the world "

" Without me, you can do nothing.
    with me, you will bear much fruit.

    but be patient
    remain in my love "

                cf John 15

" If you want to follow me
you will suffer

but be not afraid I am with you always"

" When you die, I will welcome you forever
        into the kingdom of my Father
        with Mary, my Mother
    and with all the children of my Father

        We will live together
        we will celebrate together
        together we will sing praise to my Father
        our hearts full of joy "

" But you must watch and pray,
        for Satan, the evil one
        tries to discourage you
        and to turn you away from me

        But I am with you to protect you;
        remain with me "

" Take refuge in the heart of my Father
              for he loves you
              and watches over you
              you can trust him
              for he is all-powerful in love
                        and tenderness

          he knows everything
          and not a hair falls from your head
          without his knowing it "

And JESUS tells me:

"The kingdom of my Father
is like a treasure hidden in a field
it is worth selling all you have
in order to buy it"

cf Matthew 13, 44

" The kingdom of my Father
        is like the smallest of all seeds :
     it grows in our hearts
            it becomes a tree
   where all the birds like to build their nests "

cf Matthew 13, 31

" The kingdom of my Father is like a wedding feast

to which all the poor
are invited ! "

Cf Luke 14,5

Jesus explains the beginnings
and the history of the world

cf Genesis 1

" My Father and I create all things :
      light and sun
      plants, leaves and flowers
      fish, birds and animals "

"But most important of all
          we create man and woman

The whole universe is created for them
it is their home and their garden"

" The first man and woman,
     Adam and Eve are tempted by the devil
     they disobey God
     they say to him : "no"
     they turn away from his love
     then they just look for pleasure in life
     they think only of themselves
     they no longer wish to serve "

Cf Genesis 3

"And because Adam and Eve turn away from God
and only think of themselves
they begin to fight
and their children do too

And all the men and women of the earth
begin to fight among themselves,
each one just looking for his or her own interests

there is no more love or sharing on earth
everywhere there is war, misery and hatred."

"But the Father remains faithful to his love
He has a plan for all the men and women of the earth
which is even more beautiful
for he loves them so much
and he wants them to be happy.

He is going to send them a Savior
his only beloved Son
to free their hearts
and to give them new life

and so he prepares his coming."

124

God chooses Noah
>he tells him to build an ark
>for himself, his family,
>and for all the animals, male and female

And God sends rain, rain, and more rain...
>it is a terrible flood!
>the whole earth is covered by water!

Only Noah and his family
>and the animals male and female
>who are in the ark are saved!

And God makes a covenant with Noah
>and with his children
>and with the children of his children
>with all the men and women of the earth
>he will not send another flood
>to destroy the earth.

cf Genesis 6

But once again all the men and women of the earth
        turn away from God
        everywhere there is war, misery and hatred.

God chooses Abraham
        a good and just man.

with him, his wife and his children
and the children of his children
he forms a people, the Jewish people.

God makes a covenant with them.
                    cf Genesis 15

128

The Jewish people suffer
       they become slaves, oppressed and humiliated.
       they cry out to God
       reminding him of his covenant.

And God hears the cry of his people
       he chooses Moses
       he sends him to liberate his people.
                       cf Exodus 32

After many, many years,
    the Father chooses a young girl
    MARY
    to be the mother of his beloved son

    even before her birth,
    he prepares her for this
    by creating her full of grace
                and love, all pure

    she is the immaculate one.

Mary is promised in marriage to Joseph
a good and just man
who always obeys God

The Father sends to Mary a messenger,
    The angel Gabriel
    He greets her:

        "Hail, Mary, full of grace,
        the Lord is with thee"

    He asks her to become
    the Mother of God
    She says "Yes"
        "I am the servant of the Lord
        Do with me what you want" cf Luke 1, 23-38

The Father sends his spirit to Mary
She conceives a little child: this is JESUS
The Blessed Virgin becomes the mother of God.

As soon as Mary has the baby JESUS in her
   she goes in haste to her cousin, Elizabeth

Elizabeth is also with child in her old age
Mary goes to help and serve her.

cf Luke 1, 39-56

Mary gives birth to JESUS
            in a cave in Bethleem

Joseph is there
It is Christmas

            shepherds come to adore
the Son of God who has become a little baby

                    cf Luke 2, 1-20

140

Kings come from afar
to adore him also
and to bring him gifts.

JESUS is king of Israel
king of the whole universe

cf Matthew 2

JESUS lives with Joseph and Mary
the simple family life of Nazareth

he works like everyone else
he remains there thirty years

After these thirty years
    he leaves his home, his work and his town
    to go and announce to all people
    his message of peace and love :

        the Good News

he also works miracles.
        cf John 2, 1-12

JESUS calls disciples and twelve apostles to join him
he asks them to leave everything and to come and follow him
he chooses them to continue his work
                    to preach as he preaches
                    to be good and kind as he is good and kind
                    to heal as he heals
              among the twelve apostles, there is Peter
          JESUS chooses him to be
                    the rock on which his church is built
                    the first of the apostles
                    the first pope

                    and there is John
                    whom he loves with a special love.
                              cf Matthew 4, 18-22

Today, the pope is like Peter
    he is a friend of JESUS
    the first of the bishops
    the shepherd of shepherds

he confirms the other bishops
he recalls the words of JESUS for all the Church.

Among the disciples of JESUS
there is Mary, his mother.

she is the most attentive and the most silent
she receives his word with love and joy
she keeps all things hidden in her heart
she loves and adores.

There is also Martha and Mary
the sisters of Lazarus

JESUS loves them very much
he often goes to their home to rest

cf Luke 10-38

There is a woman who lives a sinful life
JESUS looks at her with tenderness and says

   " I do not condemn you
      go your way; from now on sin no more!"

   she will not sin anymore
   for she has met JESUS
   and she knows she is loved infinitely

                              cf John 8

But others do not want JESUS
    they are frightened by his message
    they are attached to their money and their power
    they refuse to listen and to welcome his word
    they close their hearts
    they are jealous and try to trap him

On the Thursday before the Passover

JESUS gathers the apostles
to share the meal with them

he knows it is his last meal

Before eating, he washes their feet
and becomes their servant
he says to them:

"Do this to one another"

"then you will be happy and blessed of my Father"

cf John 13

160

During the meal, JESUS gives to the apostles
          his Body to eat in the form of bread
          his Blood to drink in the form of wine
          a sign of his death and of the gift of his life
               it is the first Mass, the Eucharist
He says to them: "Do this in memory of me"
he makes them priests
          Then JESUS speaks to them :
               "Love one another as I love you
                this is a new commandment
                soon I will be leaving you
                but do not let your hearts be troubled!
                I will pray the Father
                he will send you the Paraclete
                         the Holy Spirit
                you will be persecuted
                but I will be with you always"

                              cf Matthew 26
                              John 14. 15-16

Then JESUS goes to the Garden of Olives
with Peter, James and John
        he is in deep anguish and distress
        he says to them :
                " my soul is sad unto death "

He prays : " Father, not my will but yours "

cf Luke 22, 40

The enemies of JESUS want to kill him
        they use Judas
        one of the twelve apostles
he comes with soldiers
        to arrest and imprison JESUS

Judas betrays him with a kiss

Peter, the first of the apostles, is frightened
    he pretends he does not know JESUS
    he says:
            " I do not know that man ! "

        and the cock crows . . .

from afar JESUS looks at him with tenderness

        Peter weeps bitterly

        JESUS forgives
                cf Luke 22, 61

JESUS is put into prison
   he is judged
   and condemned to die on a cross
   he is struck
   and crowned with thorns
   he suffers greatly
                    cf John 19

170

He carries his cross on his shoulders
to Mount Calvary

Simon of Cyrene helps him

JeSUS falls a number of times
he suffers terribly

cf Luke 23, 26

The soldiers nail JESUS to the cross
        he is like a lamb - wounded and innocent -
        a victim to save us and to heal us

        From the cross
        JESUS gives Mary to John

        "Here is your mother"

From that moment on, John takes care of Mary
        he loves her as JESUS loves her.

                        cf John 19 ·

Jesus cries out: "I thirst!"
he gives up his spirit
he dies

a soldier pierces his heart
with a sword
from the wound flows blood and water

cf John 19

They take his body down from the cross
and give him to his mother
she receives him with love

Then they put the body into a tomb
sealed by a large stone.

On Easter Sunday

JESUS RISES FROM DEATH!
ALLELUIA!

he is living now and forever!

ALLELUIA!

Early in the morning, Mary of Magdalene goes to the tomb
      she is weeping
JESUS appears to her dressed as a gardener
      she does not recognize him
      until he calls her by her name :
          " Mary "

      she cries : " Rabboni ", " Master " !
      and throws herself at his feet.

              cf John 20, 11-18

Later JESUS appears to his apostles
     at the lake of Tiberias
     he has breakfast with them
     then he says to Peter:

          " Peter, do you love me ? "
          " Yes, says Peter, you know that I love you "
          JESUS says : " feed my lambs "

Thus JESUS confirms Peter
     as shepherd of his Church
     as the first pope.
                         cf John 21

On the day of the Ascension

      JESUS tells the apostles and disciples
      to wait and pray
      he is going to send them his spirit

Then he leaves them and goes to the Father.

cf Acts 1

On Pentecost Sunday
　　　　　　　 _ ten days after the departure of JESUS _
　　　　　　　 Mary and the apostles are together in prayer
　　　　　　　 they await the promise of JESUS

　　　 suddenly, they hear a noise
　　　 like a violent wind
　　　 and tongues as of fire

　　　　　 appear to them

　　　　　　 which rest on each one of them

And they are all filled with the Holy Spirit
　　　 a new strength rises up in them
　　　 and they begin to proclaim in various languages:

"JESUS is the Son of God, the Savior of the world"

The Church of JESUS is born and is revealed to the world

　　　　　　　　　　　　　　　　 cf Acts 2

The apostles filled with this new fire
    go off throughout the world
    to speak of JESUS
    and of his good news everywhere
    they baptize all those who believe in JESUS

"In the name of the Father, the Son and the Holy Spirit"

The family of God, the Church, grows in number

Mary lives with John
     John is her priest
     until her death

Then, like JESUS, she rises from the dead
     and enters Heaven with a glorified body

This is the Assumption!

We too will rise with glorified bodies
     at the end of time
JESUS and Mary await us in the kingdom.

The apostles die as martyrs for Jesus
  bishops replace them
      they continue to preach Jesus
      and his good news
            throughout the world
            and throughout time

  like the apostles they create
        and confirm christian communities

These communities are made up of
        families - mothers, fathers
        with their children
        and also those who are not married

  some give their lives completely to Jesus

The weak, the sick, the poor, the elderly
   - all those who are suffering and lonely -
   are at the heart of these communities

they are at the heart of the Church of Jesus

      Jesus loves them with a special love
      he chooses the weak and the little ones
      to confound the strong

Their prayer touches the heart of the Father.

In the history of the Church

JESUS calls men and women
like you and me to be saints
to live the life of the Holy Spirit
    they are friends of JESUS
    friends of the poor
    and our models
they speak of JESUS and to JESUS
they speak to the poor
they are our friends
waiting for us in Heaven.

JESUS is alive
      at the heart of his Church
he remains with us and in us.

      with him we love one another
            we create community
            we learn to forgive and to celebrate
            we welcome the poor
      we give our lives for our brothers and sisters
      and we work towards creating a more friendly world
      we are the face
            the hands and the heart of JESUS

At the heart of our communities
    we pray a lot
    and offer our difficulties and sufferings
    to the Father, in union with JESUS
    so that all the men and women
    of the earth may be saved.

And all together
> with all the Church
> with all those who suffer and weep

with Mary, mother of the Church
mother of all the men and women of the earth

we await the return of JESUS in his glory

and we cry : "COME LORD JESUS, COME!"

> Cf Apocalypse 22

" I thank you, Father
   for having hidden these things
   from the wise and clever,
   and revealed them to little ones "

cf Matthew 11, 25